TEXTS WITH GOD

ANONYMOUS

"Be not conformed to this world; but be ye transformed by the renewing of your mind, that ye may prove what is that good, and acceptable, and perfect will of God"

– Romans 12:2

It was in my Spam folder.

I wasn't a frequent user of the internet and often I could go without checking my email for weeks. I live in a one bedroom rustic cabin outside of Bennington and the only time I access the internet is when I venture into my favorite coffee shop. They have free wi-fi and a couple of old computers that people can use. If I get in early, I can often use one of them.

It was on a cool autumn day in October that I was truly enjoying my coffee and something in my head told me to check my spam folder. After all, there were very few regular emails, so I might as well entertain myself with dreams of an email from the King of Kenya that was actually legit and I was destined to live the life of wealth and fame.

On paper, my life might seem good. I had some success in business and now have enough money to live on and my life was pretty simple. Just me and Maggie, my little beagle, in a rural cabin deep in the woods of Vermont. She's sitting next to me. They let dogs into the coffee shop. Probably another reason I like this place.

It has been just me, and her since my wife, Joy died nearly three years ago.

Anyway, my point here is not to share my story. I'm here to show you what was in my spam folder.

I had no idea why I received it. In fact, I originally suspected that many people had received it. But I've yet to see it anywhere on the internet. And I've been checking. I've actually become a more regular user for just that reason.

Since I haven't seen it on the internet, I must assume that others have not received it, or if they have, they've used it for their own purposes or deleted it.

But something is telling me that it's time to share it. I've come to think that it's actually Joy instructing me to do so. I used to bristle at her advice and instructions at my eating and work habits. Now I miss them. Dearly.

So here it is. I've made no changes to it. The email address was simply JCnot666@yahoo.com. There was no name on it. It was an attachment and although most people are told not to open an attachment from someone you don't know, I did.

The title of the document was "Texts With God" and it began....

My daughter was sick. Very sick. She had been living on her own but when she got sick, she moved back home and was living with us again.

Tonight, my wife had been crying for hours. I've been laying awake in bed after comforting her, and saw that it was now 3:12 in the morning. It was clear that I wasn't going to fall asleep.

I also realized that I was angry. Very angry!

Why would God allow my daughter, who is the sweetest person alive, to suffer with a disease that will soon take her life?

I grabbed my cellphone and decided to text my anger into the great beyond. I texted the following message to a made up number:

Dear God, why do you cause bad things to happen to good people?

I know that you are a good person.

Who is this?

Who were you trying to reach?

I made up a number and actually wanted to tell God how mad I am at Him! I'm sorry to bother you.

You're not bothering me and I'd like to hear more about how you're feeling.

Look it's nice to chat but I really didn't mean to bother you. Goodbye.

Don't stop. It sounds like you need to talk to someone so tell me what's hurting you.

Well why not? If I can't get God at least I can get a friend.

God is your friend.

If He's my friend, why is He letting my daughter suffer so much?

First of all, how do you know that God is a He? But more importantly tell me about your daughter.

He. She. Whatever. My daughter was recently diagnosed with cancer and her mother and I are very distraught.

You love Sophia very much.
I know that.

How do you know her name
is Sophia?

Who were you trying to reach?

I wasn't trying to reach anybody!

I heard your prayer.

Who is this?

You've prayed in the past but
your praying has become
even more fervent lately.

Fervent?

There are things that have been written about me that I'm not that fond of, but one thing that really hit the mark was by another James when he wrote "the effectual fervent prayer of a righteous man availeth much".

I just read that last night. It was James 5:16.

Are you a righteous man, James?

Look, this is too weird. I don't know who you are or how you know this but I need to stop this now!

Please James don't.

Three days later, Sophia's reports came back and her cancer had advanced. I had always prayed since I was younger but I was praying much more, simply because I didn't know what else to do.

Then I decided to return to my texting and I redialed my texting "companion". When the phone connected, I began texting.

You really expect me to believe in something or someone that would actually take away my own child? Who did nothing to deserve this?

I know that you would expect me to go on about how I actually took my own son and expect that there's some deep Spiritual insight in that but I know that you hurt and ache.

Is this one of those Spiritual numbers where I'm going to have to accept Jesus at the end of the call?

Do you want to?

LOL Going for the close already! That's funny! LMAO.

You need to help me with those words - LOL and LMAO. What do they mean?

What did they put a really old guy on the line tonight who knows nothing about texting?

Well I am actually pretty old, but believe me, I look good for my age. What does LOL mean?

Laugh Out Loud and Laugh My Ass Off. You bible thumpers make me laugh. It's almost like you get something for everyone who says that they accept Jesus as their Lord and Savior. Well if He's such a savior, where is He while my daughter suffers?

I think that we all get something when someone accepts Jesus, but I want to know more about your daughter and if you'd like, I won't use her name this time.

What do you mean this time?

You were very upset the last time when I mentioned her name, and I'd like to stay on with you long enough for me to be of some help to you.

WTF?

You get so angry when you realize that maybe this is actually God. Don't you believe that God is always listening to you and around you?

Many times, no.

Then why did you reach out to me?

Because, I don't know where else to turn.

See this is what makes me laugh. Most people only turn to me when they don't know where else to turn. I'm always here for people and few recognize that.

You mean you can laugh?

I probably didn't put that right. You see I'm always laughing, but it's laughing with joy. In this case, I guess I meant that it makes me shake my head and be surprised.

Well you have to admit that most people aren't really sure that you actually exist.

How can that be? Look around at all of the beauty you have. Plants. Trees. Animals. Water. People. My handiwork is all around.

Well maybe you just need to announce yourself more often.

That didn't work for you. I told you that I was God and even told you that I knew your name and Sophia's and you told me WTF, which I'm not sure I want to know what that means.

Well you have to admit that when you do that, it's very strange and unexpected and hard to believe.

That's why I recommended to Jesus to speak in parables. It seems when he told others who he was, they got angry and we all know how that turned out.

But wasn't that how it was supposed to turn out?

Well, it is true that I do have a hand, ok, a big hand, in how things turn out, but why do you think it turned out that way?

I thought that you had to sacrifice your son to atone for the sins of all.

Would you do that with your daughter?

Probably not, but you're God, not me!

James, I have to admit that this is one that I've found baffling. I would sacrifice my son to pay for everyone's sins. Pay to whom?

I guess to you. I was always led to believe that you needed a blood sacrifice to make up for the sins started by Adam.

Ah, Adam. You would think that he should also be considered my son. No?

I guess.

And would Eve be my daughter? Wow, then it really gets messy by today's standards right? Not many other options when you're the first two people around however.

So was Adam your son like Jesus was your son?

James, everyone is my son and everyone is my daughter. I've been trying to make that clear for so long and it still feels like people don't understand that.

But Jesus was your only begotten son and you sent Him here to save us!

Of course I sent Jesus to save others. But everyone has the ability to save others. What was Jesus' best line?

Best line?

Well, what I mean is what was the main commandment that he taught?

Love your God with all your heart.

Well yes, yes that one, of course. He really was a good son. If all of my sons and daughters believed that, the world would be as I intended. What was the other one?

To love your neighbor as you love yourself?

Yes. Many of you call that the golden rule. But I've found that many of you don't follow rules, even if I call them golden.

I always found that one somewhat interesting. What happens to those who don't love themselves?

Think of it this way - I created you. Everything I created, I love. No matter what shape or condition. My creation is perfect to me. The love I give to everything is perfect as well. But often, as many of you like to say, life gets in the way.

Yea, life gets in the way! How about when someone is handicapped? Or they're abused and they learn to hate themselves and hate life? How can they love others when it's hard to just love themselves and the life they're forced to live?

Well, that can be true. In order to love one another, you have to love yourself. It is very hard to love something else if you do not love yourself. But loving others does begin from within yourself. And it's within that people can find me.

I'm not sure that I understand that.

Think of this. When you see a puppy or a new born baby, or if you're angry at that moment, maybe even mad at me, we all know that that happens, but if you are, do you show this anger on the puppy or the baby?

When you're feeling upset or angry, your ability to still feel love and compassion is always within you. You just need to let me take over and not the feelings that are being caused by the outside world.

How can I not let the outside world bother me? Do you see the things that are happening? War. Anger amongst neighbors. Murder in the street. Where are you when this is going on?

I'm always within everyone involved. People let the outside world take them over and they push me aside. This is when they do things that can cause damage to others.

Is that when the devil comes into play?

Devil? I love this one. The images range from an evil twin to a serpent with a tail. I have to break it to you - There's only me.

There's no devil?

Oh, what you call the devil is actually all around, but it's not an entity like me or like you. It's actually the pull of the material world on us.

But you created the material world?

I created a world that would give everyone everything they need. Remember that saying about how even the birds have all they need and all the clothes they need?

I gave everyone all that they needed, but for many they didn't see the love that came with it, and they decided that they wanted more than was provided and weren't willing to share the love I gave them as well.

But if you created everyone, why didn't you make it understood to everyone that they didn't have to worry about having more than others?

Because you're my creations. I gave you many wonderful qualities. Most of them people don't even use. Don't get me started on that.

Instead people focused on the things around them that brought their bodies pleasure and then they made up troubles and lies that brought them pain.

Oh, the body. Are you going to discuss your problems with sex?

No, no, sex is fine. In fact people get too hung up on the sex stuff when they think of what's right and what's wrong.

The sex was intended for reproduction and I know that that gave some additional benefits as well. But the main thing is that the primary feeling that people should feel is the love for each other and for me.

So if it was all about reproducing, then I guess you don't like this same sex stuff?

The question is not about sex or male or female. It's about the love. Let me ask you, if two people of the same sex are in love and treating each other and those around them with love, do you think they're less to me than the man and woman couple who treat others with hatred and don't display the Love that I gave them?

I guess I can understand that.

You see, what I mean when I say it's not about the sex, I mean it's not about the focus on the needs of the physical world.

That's when people focus on themselves and the world outside. I care about what's on the inside of each of us. The love I gave them to share. To love themselves and to love others.

Well what about what you said regarding the body and what brings it pleasure?

Do you like to eat? Everyone does. In fact the way the body works you need to. That's why I gave the world enough for everyone and all time. However, in the physical world, how do you get food now?

You buy it. What happens if you can't pay for food that you really like? You do without or you steal it from others? Should it be man or me who controls what you eat?

So are you saying that selling food is no good? That business is no good? Seems if that was so, the world would be chaos.

Chaos? That's a man made word. It's not something I created. I don't think that business is bad.

It has allowed many people to succeed and thrive in this world and I've been there to help many to do so. But business makes things better for all when its goals are to help, not hurt others.

But I've always been taught that business is a zero sum game - someone wins and someone loses.

Do you think that I created this world for it to be a place where some win and some lose? That's where things go wrong with that kind of thinking.

I created a world where all can, as you say, win. I think of it a bit differently, but I certainly never intended that any of my creations would lose.

Well there are plenty of poor people who seem to be losing.

In this world, yes it seems that they are. But in the only world that truly exists, no one is losing.

Wait a minute, you say in this world, but this is the world we live in.

Is it? When you sleep, do you feel part of this world? When you quiet your mind and think beyond what's around you, do you feel part of this world? Do you believe that this world that you live in now is all there is?

I certainly hope not.

And you hope not because of Sophia right?

I need to know that there's something more than this – there's too much pain here. If you saw the pain that Sophia endures, you'd understand!

I do see that pain. Let me ask you, when you pray, do you ask for me to take away the pain from Sophia?

Of course, she's my child!

What prayer do you use when you pray to me?

The Lord's Prayer. I was taught that when I was a kid and say it every night. Not sure how well it's ever worked. Look at my Sophia!

You learned that prayer from The Bible right? In it, Luke speaks about the prayer and then what does he talk about?

I don't know, I'd have to look it up. Wait, it's Luke, chapter 11.

After Luke tells the Lord's Prayer, he tells of a parable about a man who asks for three loaves of bread from a friend at midnight because he has a guest at his house.

Yes I have it here. That always seemed to be a strange story given that it follows a part that is probably one of the most widely known readings in the Book.

There are many strange stories in that Book, I must admit. Just like the man at the door was, you have been persistent and fervent in your prayers to me about Sophia. I have heard your prayers and am here.

This is the part of the Bible where it also says that good parents don't give their kids stones when they ask for bread.

And it says 'how much shall your heavenly Father give the Holy Spirit to them that ask him?'

Well I'm praying and asking, and she's still sick. And getting worse.

What do you pray for? For her body to get better?

Yes, of course!

If you believe that you're speaking to God right now, tell me how do you feel? Do you feel pain? Do you even feel your own body?

What do you mean? I'm not sick!

When you pray, don't focus on the needs of the body or the things of this world. Pray like you're speaking to me right now.

Pray that you may be one with me and talk like we're talking right now. And most importantly, pray not for the things of this world that you see but what you don't see.

I don't understand. So many times I pray for things of this world to be better, not just for me, but for everyone. Isn't that the right thing?

When you pray and seek the Spirit rather than the physical world, your message gets to me and helps to heal all.

But what I know is the physical world.

What are you thinking about right now?

Right now? My daughter getting better!

By praying, are you asking the physical world or the Spiritual world for that to happen?

I'm asking you and you don't seem to be listening!!!! I need to go.

I stayed away from texting for about 2 weeks. My daughter's condition seemed to stay steady and she suddenly seemed more at peace with things. She was smiling and actually had started to read and listen to music again. My wife and I noted this to her doctor and he agreed that she seemed to be in a better mental state. He credited it to the normal stages that people take in this condition but it seemed to me that there was something more than just a "normal" stage.

One night, I was with Sophia and we were chatting about the music she was listening to. She loved jazz, which I played her when she was a child. In an effort to connect as much as possible with my daughter, I had begun to brush up on my knowledge of jazz and this helped our conversations. After we had a good laugh about how I couldn't understand the difference between Art Pepper's music and Gerry Mulligan, she turned to me and said, "Keep texting."

"What did you say?" I asked.

"Keep texting Daddy, with your new friend. It's helping. Both of us."

Before I got the chance to ask her to explain, my wife came in with her medicine and it was time for Sophia to rest.

Later that evening, I texted my "new friend".

Alright, I need some answers. Who are you?

Who do you think I am?

Look whoever you are, I don't know how you did it, but I don't want you communicating with Sophia!

James, before you get so angry, tell me what makes Sophia the love of your life?

No, I'm asking the questions here! I want to know how she knows that we're texting each other?

Sophia and I chat all the time. Oh of course, we don't use phones or texting, but she speaks with me many times a day. Do you think Sophia prays?

I don't know for sure, but I had hoped that she did.

She's been praying to me since she was a kid. I must admit that she's much more consistent at it than you are.

Well if she's praying to you, why don't you make her better?

Did she seem better to you today?

Better? SHE HAS CANCER! SHE'S DYING!!!!!!!!!!!!!!!!!!

What does dying mean to you James?

It means that she'll be taken away from me.

Like your Mom was taken away from you when you were younger?

How do you know about my Mom?

Even though it may seem a long time for you, do you still feel your Mom around you at times?

I see her in my dreams. I see her in Sophia. Are you saying that she's with you now?

Everyone is with me. Always.

But my Mom wasn't a believer. She left the church when she married my Dad. Said she had no use for a church that did bad things to people.

My Dad was a Baptist and even though he tried as hard as he could, she wouldn't accept Jesus and he was sad when she died and believed that she wouldn't go to Heaven.

The church? The world is my church. I remember reading something that someone wrote that "God gave us the Spirit, but the devil gave us religion"

Even though I chuckle at the devil image, I always thought that statement was pretty valid given many of the crazy things that I've seen people try to connect with me under the guise of a "church".

So what church is your church?

The church of Love and everyone is a part of it.

Is it a Christian church?

When Jesus was on the earth, was it more important for him to deliver His message or to create a church and a religion?

I guess his message?

What was his message James?

To love others.

OK. What did he teach?

He taught us to love others.

What else did he do?

He rose from the dead.

That's always what people say. Everyone says that he taught us to love each other and he rose from the dead. And yet both things seem to be impossible for us to do.

Well of course, he was Jesus! Your son!

But you're my son James, as well.

Whoa, you can't be putting me at the same level as Jesus, can you?

But Jesus experienced everything that man does. He loved. He cried. He was troubled by what he saw. Don't you feel these things as well?

But he rose from the dead.

He also spent most of his time healing others. Most people seem to forget that. He even brought people back to life. Was he a man or God when he did that?

Well that's what's special about him. He was both.

Do you believe that I created him or that he was part of who I am?

I guess both.

What if I told you that you were the same? That Sophia was the same? That your wife is the same? That the neighbor down the street who you don't like is the same?

But Jesus did miracles - he rose from the dead!

He gave his disciples the ability to heal as well. When he healed others, he told them that it was one's faith that heals. If you have faith, you can be healed. So doesn't that mean that everyone has the power to heal?

Well, I guess so. He did preach that we should be perfect as our Father in heaven is perfect. Can we really do that?

Is that a question for me or for you?

It's so hard to live in this world and see the injustice and evil and just turn the other cheek, or have the ability to love someone who we know is bad and evil.

Of course it's hard, but is it impossible? Let's just think about a world in which everyone did love each other. Would it be a better world?

Well, of course.

You talked about your Mom and how your father didn't think she would go to Heaven. When she died, what do you think happened to her?

I believe that she is in Heaven!

Even though your father believes that she didn't because she hadn't accepted Jesus? If you believe that, how can you believe that she's in Heaven?

Because she was a wonderful woman who loved me, and my father, and so many other people.

Yes, your Mom loved and helped many people. And whether she, as you say, accepted Jesus, I saw all of that.

So is she in Heaven?

I'm not sure what you mean by Heaven, but she's with me now. As is her Mom and her Dad.

So even those who don't accept Jesus still go to Heaven?

Like I said, what you think of as Heaven may be different from what it really is, but if it means that people are with me, then yes.

Believe me when I tell you that when people pass from your world, it doesn't take them long to accept the reality that Jesus provided a path to me and that love is the most powerful Spirit that runs through everyone and everything.

So the criminal and the killer get to go to Heaven as well?

Do you believe that I created the criminal and the killer? See, this is where your image of Heaven gets in the way. Do you think that everyone still has their same body and attitude that they had on earth when they're here with me?

Their own body? I hope that won't be the case for me! LOL.

That is funny. Like I told you, bodies don't mean anything to me. It's your Spirit and your Soul that matters. Because we are all connected to the same Spirit and same Soul.

In simple terms, when we're done with our bodies, we simply return fully to the Spirit. That's how you should envision Heaven. Not as something that is constrained by what you know, but by what exists in your heart.

I'd like to think that there's a Heaven.

Because you want your Mom and Dad to be in a safe place. A place where they can still have an impact on you. Believe me, just as they are part of me, they are part of you today and every day. Don't you feel them helping you in every decision that you make?

I don't feel them all of the time, but I do know that I often hear my Mom when I'm thinking of making a decision or when I pray.

When you pray? Of course you do. Her Spirit is always around you. Always there to help guide you. When you quiet your mind from the troubles of this world and pray, you are hearing her. But she's always there to guide you, as I am.

Is that what Jesus meant by the Holy Spirit?

Now you're getting it James.

So what will happen to Sophia?

First of all, I want you to think of Sophia only in the here and now. Do everything you can for her now. The present is the only thing that you can control for her.

So you're saying I can't control what will happen?

No I didn't say that. All I'm saying is that you should do what you can for her now. It's the present that matters. The past is done. Let the future take care of itself. All you can control is what you do now.

So you know what's going to happen? Do you know what's going to happen all of the time?

That's what people think, but actually I don't have control of everything that happens. I do know how things will end up and I can often influence things but you people here have more power than you know.

So can I save her?

What do you mean by saving her?

I want her to live!

She's alive now. Believe me, no matter what happens to her, she'll always be alive in you and alive in your wife. Think of how your Mom feels alive to you even though she's not physically with you.

That's because she's always alive with me and part of the Spiritual world that we're all actually a part of as well.

But I want Sophia here with us. I want to see her smile. I want to hug her whenever she's around. I want to watch her get older.

You can do all of those things with her now. I can't tell you what will happen to her, but I can tell you that every day that she's with you is a gift.

Every day that we have that we can feel love for others is a gift. If more people realized that we'd have more love among people and the troubles of this world would cease to exist.

Why can't you tell me what will happen to her? If you're God, you should be able to do that!

If I told you what would happen to her, would that change how you treat her and love her today? No one on your world knows what will happen tomorrow. I intended it to be that way, because I want you to live in the present. To love others now. To be present in the world now.

But right now, she's dying! And my wife and I are hurting so badly!

I know that. I also know that your daughter is alive and doesn't she seem to be in better state of mind lately?

Is that because you're communicating with her?

I told you before that I am. She feels sad for you and your wife as well. Don't you think that she wants you to feel better? She knows that you're sad. But you're making it harder on yourself by only focusing on what's going to happen to her rather than being with her now.

But I want to take care of her, and want to be sure that she'll be okay, no matter what happens to her!

James, I promise that I will take care of her. No matter what happens to her, I will be there for her. Haven't I proven that to you?

Proven? What have you proven to me? You took my Mom and Dad and now you're taking my daughter. Take me and leave my daughter. That would prove things!

Everyone is looking for proof. You say that I had my only son killed to prove that I love my people. Why can't you all just see that I show my love every day to all with the wonders around them?

New babies. Beautiful flowers and animals. Food and Water plenty. You have my love all around you and yet the proof always needs to involve death. Jesus rose from his physical body and is with me, and all of us now.

He always has been and will be in the Spirit that's part of everyone and everything. He's with you and everyone every day. If only everyone realized that, you'd all be in a better place.

You see that's what I don't get - how is He with me every day?

When you look at Sophia, do you physically feel something, or is the feeling you get from your Spirit and Soul swelling with love? When you take care of your wife and her sadness, are you doing it for her or for yourself?

When Jesus left your place, he told you all that the Holy Spirit would come. Think of what you feel when you feel love. That's the Holy Spirit. It runs throughout everyone and everything.

But we can't feel it or touch it, so how do we know it's real?

Do you only feel things that you can touch with your physical bodies?

No, I guess not.

How much time do you spend worrying and thinking about the things of the physical world?

Do you think if people spent that much time focusing on the things of the Spirit and how to make others recognize the gifts of the Spirit, the world would be a better place?

I guess so.

It is so, because then we all get closer to the Spiritual world, which is actually the only world there is.

The only world? Sorry to say this but WTF?

What you consider the physical world is really only temporary. What people perceive in this world is that here things are born and then they die.

But everything in the Spiritual world is eternal and believe me, each of us has a Spirit that is eternal as well. In fact, our Spirits are all part of just one Spirit and that's the Spiritual world.

Well if everyone lives and dies here, how can we be eternal as well?

My love for everyone and everything is eternal, and that's why when you seek oneness with the Spirit instead of the things of this world you actually get closer to the Spiritual world, which is eternal.

What is the Spiritual world?

It's the place where we're all healed and all anyone recognizes is good because the only feeling is love. In the physical world there are too many other feelings that crowd out this reality.

Was the physical world created when Adam and Eve ate the apple?

In a way, yes. That's always been an interesting story, and you should think of it less as something that really happened, and more as something that shows the split between the world I intended which is filled with only love and oneness, and the one that allowed the physical world to create so many troubles and thoughts that have ruled man since.

So that's why Jesus came – to reconnect us with that world?

Jesus came to show us how to heal the world we're in and how to heal each and every person. This healing begins by focusing on the Spirit and not the physical world you believe that you exist in.

So what is this? All a dream? LOL.

That's surely one way of looking at it. After all, I didn't create a world with wars, with illness, with cancer.

That is the physical world that man created. All the lies and thoughts that man has in his mind have created this world that you now view yourself and your daughter Sophia in.

So her cancer isn't real? Every doctor seems to think so!

And you pray that she gets better?

Of course I do!

When you pray from now on, focus on the Spirit and the love that exists between Sophia, you and everyone in the Spiritual world, which is the only true world.

Don't focus on her physical needs and the things of this world. That is the way you will heal her and heal yourself.

She has tried every medication and drug the doctors have given her. If you think that she'll get better because of the power of the mind or positive thinking, you're crazy!

It's not the power of the physical mind. Think of it as connecting with the mind that is all around and within the Spirit.

Think of it as the Divine or Spiritual mind. When you do that, you'll realize that it's the only mind and only true world that does exist.

I'm afraid that if I just do that, I'll still lose her in this world and I need to be with her, hug her, kiss her, take care of her.

No matter what happens to Sophia in your world, she will always be part of the Spirit that's within all of us.

You have many religions there, but if you look at them, the one thing that is true about them is that they ultimately focus on a Spirit-based power that exists in everyone and can heal everyone if people believe in it.

So let it heal my Sophia!

Healing her physical body is not what I'm talking about. Doesn't everyone ultimately shed their human body? You call it death.

When Jesus rose I thought it would clearly prove to you that the connection to me is not with the body, but with the Spirit. I guess sometimes even I can't make a point.

It's okay - maybe you're only human after all LOL.

God I hope not! LMAO I guess if I was human I'd have an ass.

I always knew that God had a sense of humor!

If humor brings joy and happiness to people, then yes I do.

So humor is part of the Spirit as well?

You really are catching on now James.

So what am I to do?

It's time to go back to Sophia and your wife and enjoy every moment you have with them. Slow yourself down from the troubles of your world and just feel the connection that you have with them.

Pray as I have told you to. I promise that if you do that, every minute of your life will be wonderful and joyous. Live in the present. The future will take care of itself. I will take care of you.

But I worry about Sophia.

And you fear that she will no longer be with you?

Yes, of course!

James, there's no such thing as fear. There's only Love. I gave you everything you need when I created you. Jesus came to show you that there's no reason to fear.

If you take away the fear that you have and put your trust in me, you will feel the love and abundance that I gave to all of my creations.

Do this, and believe that I will take care of her, you and your wife, no matter what! You will always feel Sophia in your heart no matter where she is.

Will she be an angel?

Well actually, I do have angels. The work of the Holy Spirit is not easy. You people are pretty stubborn and thick headed, so yes, I must enlist angels to help you experience the love of the Spirit.

So will Sophia be an angel?

Those who recognize the beauty and power of the Spirit do become angels.

So only good people become angels?

You asked me earlier if even criminals and killers are in heaven.

I want you to know that when they get here, they quickly realize what the Spirit was trying to tell them and how they missed it, and in your world they followed a different path. When they realize this, sometimes they become my best angels.

Is that what you mean by not judging people?

I made everyone good and perfect. What they do in your world depends upon the decisions they make. This is often that thing that people refer to as free will. However, everyone ultimately comes home.

When Sophia comes home as you say, will you still let her visit her Mom and Dad?

If you allow her to, she will. That I promise you.

I don't know what else to say. Whether you are who you say you are or not, you've made my head spin.

What will you do now?

I'm going to focus on taking care of Sophia and my wife, and enjoy each and every moment with Sophia.

And don't forget to pray as I told you and do so fervently. This doesn't mean that you do it loud and long. Rather praying fervently means that you trust me and place your concerns in my hands.

I will.

You have been given a gift that everyone has access to, but most don't recognize. You can set an example for others that will help you, Sophia, and so many others.

A gift?

Gifts were meant to be shared. They are answers to a prayer, or to a wish. When your Mom died, what did you wish?

I wished that I had spent more time with her before she died.

Your Mom knows that.

Is my Mom my angel?

. . .

Hello?

· ·

Hello?

Later that night, I tried dialing the number again but I didn't get another response.

This was the end of the file.

It's now three months from when I placed this on the internet. I don't know how many people have read it and I'm not even sure why I did or what it all means.

Sometimes I do think that it was really intended for me. As I mentioned, I lost my wife Joy nearly three years ago. She left me before we had the chance to have children and I soon found myself alone. Very alone. That is, except for my constant companion, Maggie, my dog. Now the two of us live in the rustic cabin Joy and I bought five years ago. Now it's a place where I could be alone and try to get my life back together.

I do admit that I find myself often speaking to Joy. I used to think that I was going crazy and this was all part of the grieving process. Many times we discussed how I wanted to join her and take my own life to do that. Somehow, I never did that. Often I felt that it was Joy telling me not to. I thought that that was just part of the process, or probably just me going crazy.

After I found the file, I must admit that I've spent more time being still, quiet, more at peace and trying not to evaluate the discussions that I'm having with Joy. I began to think that maybe there's something more than just it being part of the process, or about me 'cracking up'.

I don't know if Joy is my angel but although I miss her every day, I do feel her presence with me more than before I opened the file. Maybe a scientist or doctor would have an explanation for it, but I know that I'm just a simple guy who loved his wife and lost her well before we had a chance to build a long life together.

I do admit that I even tried to pray as James was instructed. I found that when I focused on trusting God and the Spiritual world mentioned in the texts, I actually felt closer to Joy and the problems of this world seemed to become smaller. It's helped me to feel that even when I'm not praying, it seems that she's here with me. Maybe it's through a connection to what was called in James' texts, the Spiritual world or the divine Mind. All I know is that I feel better and more alive than I did.

So now I find myself coming to this coffee shop every day. I do talk to more people every day. I smile when I come in and have even started to talk to, and help others, including some older folks who come in regularly and like me to read the daily paper to them.

In fact, I need to go now as one of my new friends has come into the shop. She's not one of the older folks and she can read the paper just fine, but we'll have coffee and we end up talking and laughing together. A lot!

Maggie likes her and I know that Joy would love her as well.

Her name is Sophia.

PUBLISHER'S NOTE:

When we first encountered the manuscript for this book, we were unsure if it was the kind of book that we would publish.

After reading it a few times, it reminded me of the impact that books like "Jonathan Livingston Seagull" and "The Shack" had on me.

We're proud to publish this book and hope that it's impacted you as well. If so, we ask that you share the book with others. Pass it on! The goal is to share its message with others.

If you'd like to share your thoughts and comments on the book, please visit the site:

http://www.TextsWithGod.com

Thanks.

www.ingramcontent.com/pod-product-compliance
Lightning Source LLC
Chambersburg PA
CBHW071845020426
42331CB00007B/1859